For Janine
A very happy Birthday...
We love you very much...
Marwa
Inge
♥ Dahlia
2005

Jane Walker
Consultant: Richard Tames

Miles Kelly
PUBLISHING

First published in 2002 by
Miles Kelly Publishing Ltd
Bardfield Centre, Great Bardfield, Essex, CM7 4SL

Copyright © Miles Kelly Publishing 2002
2 4 6 8 10 9 7 5 3 1

Some material in this book can also be found in *100 Things You Should Know About Ancient Egypt.*

Editor: Amanda Learmonth

Design: Debbie Meekcoms

Index: Lynn Bresler

Art Director: Clare Sleven

Editorial Director: Paula Borton

British Library Cataloguing-in-Publication Data
A catalogue record for this book is available from the British Library

ISBN 1-84236-105-8

Printed in Hong Kong

www.mileskelly.net
info@mileskelly.net

ACKNOWLEDGEMENTS

The Publishers would like to thank the following artists who have contributed to this book:
Vanessa Card, Mike Foster (Maltings Partnership), Terry Gabbey (AFA), Peter Gregory, Richard Hook (Linden Artists Ltd.), John James (Temple Rogers), Janos Marffy, Roger Payne, Terry Riley, Eric Rowe (Linden Artists Ltd.), Peter Sarson, Rob Sheffield, Nick Spender, Graham Sumner (Specs Art), Mike Taylor, Rudi Vizi, Mike White (Temple Rogers)

Computer-generated cartoons by James Evans

Contents

Life on the Nile

Without the waters of the river Nile, Egyptian civilization might never have existed. The Nile provided water for drinking, watering crops and for transport. Over 7000 years ago, people from central Africa began to arrive in Egypt and settle along the banks of the Nile.

Boats were the best way to get around.

Papyrus reeds had many uses, from making boats to shoes.

Temples were built to worship the Egyptian gods.

Powerful pharaohs

The rulers of ancient Egypt were called pharaohs. The word 'pharaoh' means great house. The pharaoh was the most important and powerful person in the country. He owned all the land and ordinary people believed that he was a god.

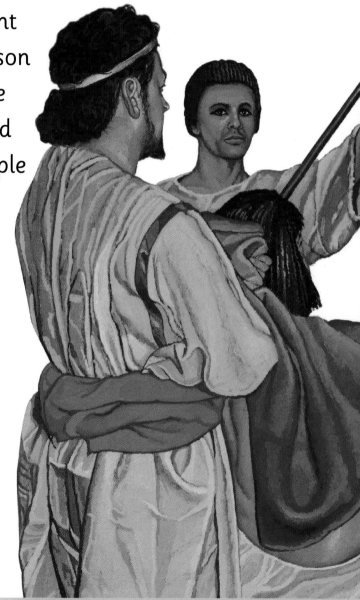

▶ These people are paying tribute to the pharaoh. This means that they have come to give him presents and tell him how great he is!

◄ Here the pharaoh is holding the symbols of his rule, the hook and flail.

Ramses II ruled for over 60 years. He was a great builder and a brave soldier.

Tutankhamun was only nine years old when he became pharaoh.

Cleo's fun facts!

Women courtiers sometimes wore hair cones made of scented animal fat. When it melted it made their hair sweet-smelling – and greasy!

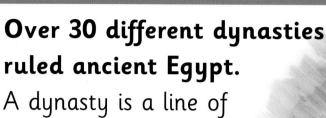

Over 30 different dynasties ruled ancient Egypt.
A dynasty is a line of rulers from the same family. The pharaoh often married a sister or half-sister, so that the blood of the royal family remained pure.

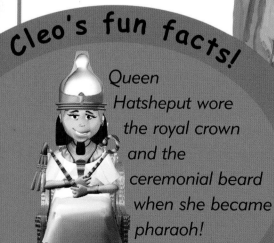

Cleo's fun facts!

Queen Hatsheput wore the royal crown and the ceremonial beard when she became pharaoh!

▼ Cleopatra was one of the last rulers of Egypt. She fell in love with Roman general, Julius Caesar, and later married Mark Antony (shown here).

Queen Hatshepsut ruled Egypt for 20 years.

Pepi II ruled Egypt for 94 years – the longest reign in history!

The two royal crowns were worn together.

9

Gods and goddesses

The ancient Egyptians worshipped more than 1000 different gods and goddesses. The most important god of all was Re, the sun god. People believed that he was swallowed up each evening by the sky goddess Nut. During the night Re travelled through the underworld and was born again each morning.

Re

Isis

Osiris

Horus

Test your memory!

1. How many years ago did the first settlers arrive in Egypt?
2. What does the word 'pharaoh' actually mean?
3. How old was Tutankhamun when he became pharaoh?
4. Who did Cleopatra marry?

1. over 7000 years ago *2.* great house *3.* nine years old *4.* Mark Antony

Horus was the god of the sky, and had the head of a hawk.

Osiris and Isis were in charge of the underworld.

Anubis

Anubis, the jackal god, watched over the dead.

The great pyramids

The three pyramids at Giza are more than 4500 years old. They were built for three kings: Khufu, Khafre and Menkaure. After the kings died, their bodies were preserved as mummies and buried inside the pyramids. Many pyramids still stand today. The biggest one of all, the Great Pyramid, took more than 20 years to build.

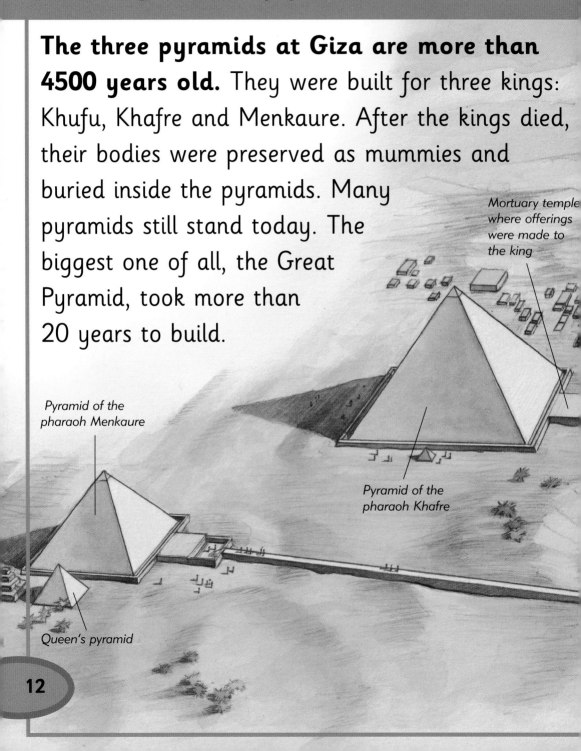

Mortuary temple where offerings were made to the king

Pyramid of the pharaoh Menkaure

Pyramid of the pharaoh Khafre

Queen's pyramid

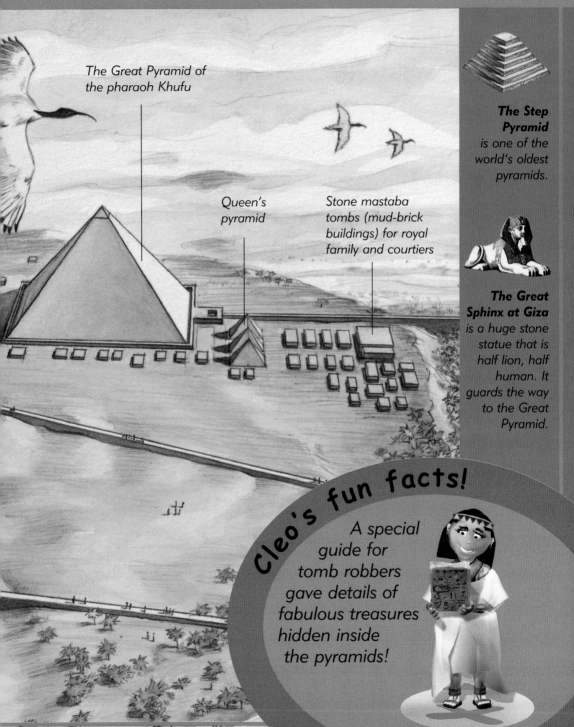

The Great Pyramid of the pharaoh Khufu

Queen's pyramid

Stone mastaba tombs (mud-brick buildings) for royal family and courtiers

The Step Pyramid is one of the world's oldest pyramids.

The Great Sphinx at Giza is a huge stone statue that is half lion, half human. It guards the way to the Great Pyramid.

Cleo's fun facts!

A special guide for tomb robbers gave details of fabulous treasures hidden inside the pyramids!

The Valley of the Kings

From about 2150BC, pharaohs were not buried in pyramids, but in tombs in the Valley of the Kings. The tombs were cut into the cliffs, or built deep underground.

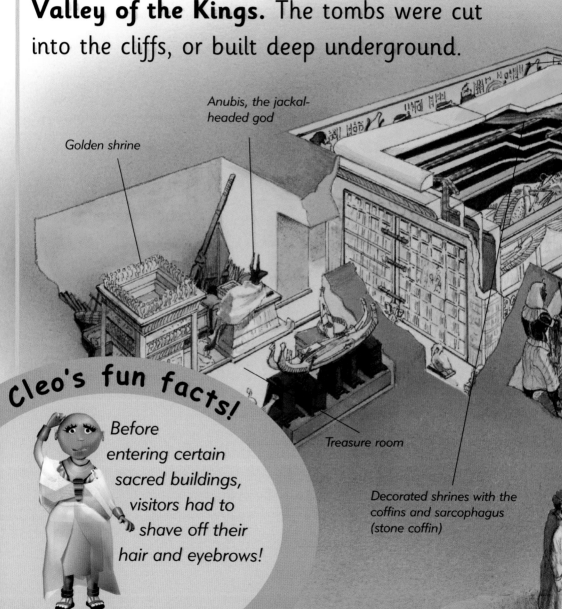

Anubis, the jackal-headed god

Golden shrine

Treasure room

Decorated shrines with the coffins and sarcophagus (stone coffin)

Cleo's fun facts!

Before entering certain sacred buildings, visitors had to shave off their hair and eyebrows!

▼ The tomb of Tutankhamun, the boy king, was discovered in 1922. It was the only tomb left in the Valley of the Kings which was not completely destroyed by robbers.

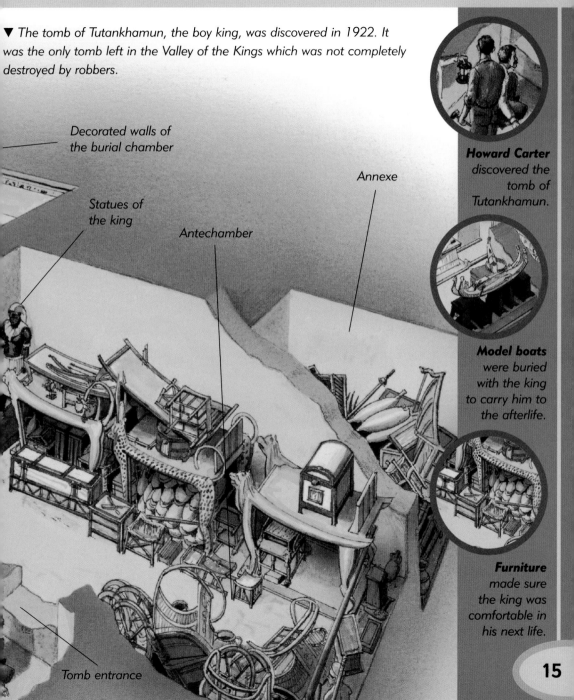

Decorated walls of the burial chamber

Statues of the king

Antechamber

Annexe

Tomb entrance

Howard Carter discovered the tomb of Tutankhamun.

Model boats were buried with the king to carry him to the afterlife.

Furniture made sure the king was comfortable in his next life.

How to make a mummy

Making a mummy was skilled work.
The body's insides were removed,
except for the heart. Next, the
body was left to dry for 40 days.
Then it was washed and
filled with linen to
keep its shape.
Finally, the body was
oiled and wrapped in
linen bandages.

Wooden coffin for the body

Make a death mask

You will need
- a play mask (made of plastic or card)
- PVA glue
- a paintbrush
- newspaper
- poster paints
- white paint

1. Cover the mask in PVA glue.
2. Tear the newspaper into strips. Layer the strips over the mask and leave to dry.
3. Cover the mask with white paint. Leave to dry.
4. Use the paints to create your own death mask!

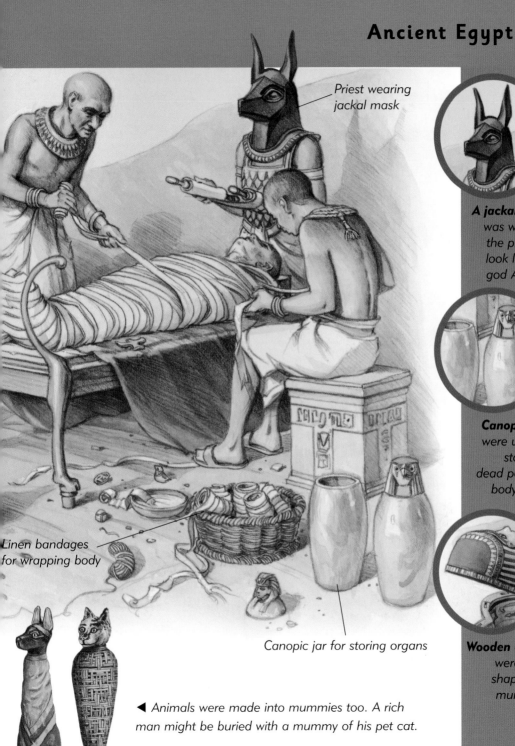

Priest wearing jackal mask

A jackal mask was worn by the priest to look like the god Anubis.

Canopic jars were used to store the dead person's body parts.

Wooden coffins were often shaped like mummies.

Linen bandages for wrapping body

Canopic jar for storing organs

◄ Animals were made into mummies too. A rich man might be buried with a mummy of his pet cat.

17

War and weapons

Egypt created a professional army of trained soldiers. The pharaoh was in charge of this army, and led his soldiers into battle.

▼ Specially trained soldiers fired arrows from horse-drawn chariots like this. The Egyptians defeated many enemies this way.

Foot soldiers carried a strong shield and a long, deadly spear.

Warships were used to defeat invaders from the sea.

Cleo's fun facts!

Soldiers who fought bravely in battle were awarded golden fly medals – for 'stinging' the enemy so successfully!

Buying and selling

Egyptian traders did not use money to buy and sell goods. Instead they exchanged goods with foreign traders. This was called bartering. Merchants visited nearby countries and offered things such as gold, a kind of paper called papyrus and cattle. In return they were given goods such as silver, cedar wood and ivory.

▼ An ancient Egyptian town had its own market place, where people went to buy food, pots, pans and other everyday goods.

Egyptians took their goods to market to exchange for other items.

Market stalls sold all kinds of fruits and vegetables.

Cleo's fun facts!

Fly swatters made from giraffe tails were a popular fashion item in ancient Egypt.

Farming the land

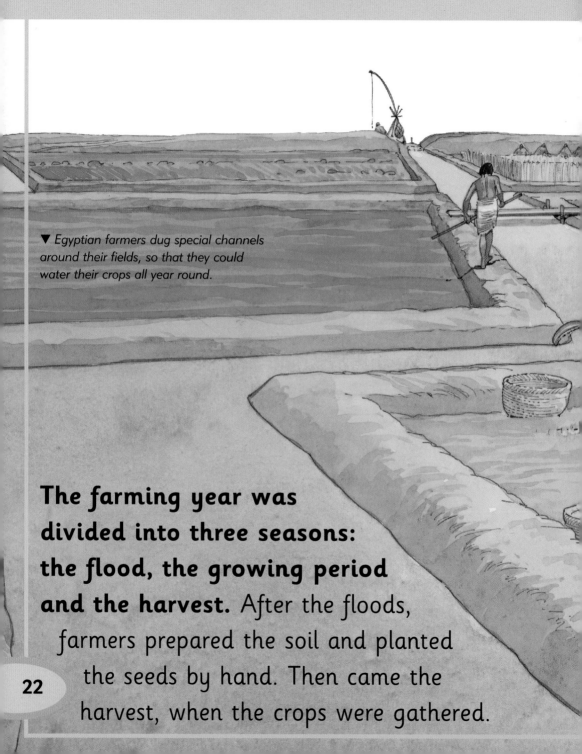

▼ Egyptian farmers dug special channels around their fields, so that they could water their crops all year round.

The farming year was divided into three seasons: the flood, the growing period and the harvest. After the floods, farmers prepared the soil and planted the seeds by hand. Then came the harvest, when the crops were gathered.

▼ Workers gathered the grain by throwing the grain and chaff (grain shell) into the air so that the heavier grain dropped to the floor.

Fruits and vegetables grew well in the strips of rich, dark soil.

A shaduf was a device used for lifting water from the Nile.

Cleo's fun facts!

Sometimes farmers hired flute players to keep people company while they worked.

Sailing around

The main method of transport in ancient Egypt was by boat along the river Nile.
The Nile is the world's longest river. It flows across the entire length of the desert lands of Egypt. The earliest boats were made from papyrus reeds. Gradually, wooden boats replaced them.

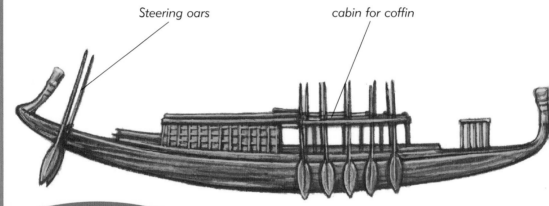

Steering oars

cabin for coffin

Cleo's fun facts!

In 1970, a Norwegian explorer sailed a papyrus boat all the way from North Africa to the Caribbean!

▲ A special carved boat was built to carry the body of King Khufu at his funeral. It was buried in a special pit next to the Great Pyramid.

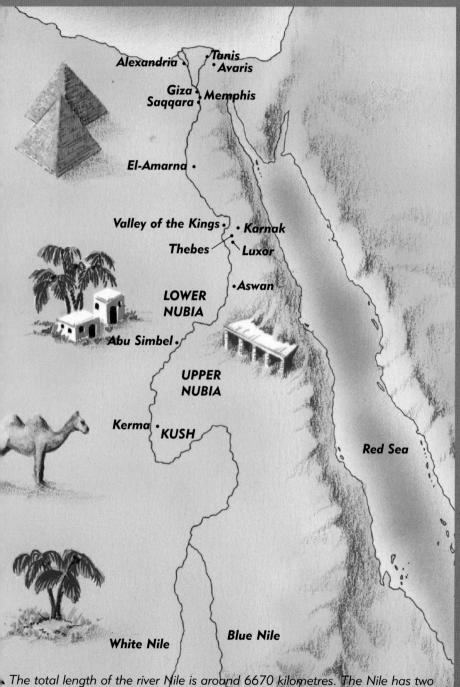

Alexandria •
• Tanis
• Avaris

Giza •
Saqqara • • Memphis

El-Amarna •

Valley of the Kings •
• Karnak
Thebes
• Luxor

• Aswan

LOWER NUBIA

Abu Simbel •

UPPER NUBIA

Kerma • • **KUSH**

Red Sea

White Nile

Blue Nile

Early boats were made from bundles of reeds tied together.

Trading ships used both sail and oar power.

Wooden barges carried building blocks across the river for the pyramids and temples.

The total length of the river Nile is around 6670 kilometres. The Nile has two main branches – the White Nile and the Blue Nile

25

Life at home

Egyptian houses were made from mud bricks dried in the sun. The inside walls were covered with thick plaster, which helped keep the houses cool in the hot weather. Wealthy Egyptians lived in villas in the countryside. Poorer families lived mostly in towns or villages, often in a crowded single room.

The walls inside the home were often decorated with paintings

Senet was a popular board game

Test your memory!

1. Who was in charge of the Egyptian army?
2. Which part of the body was left inside a mummy?
3. What is the name of the device used for lifting water?
4. What were the earliest boats made from?

1. the pharaoh 2. the heart 3. shaduf 4. papyrus reeds

Mud
was shaped
into bricks
and left to dry
in the sun.

Oil lamps
made of clay
were used
as lights.

**The dwarf
god, Bes,**
was the
Egyptian god
of the home.

The Egyptian
used papyrus mats
instead of carpets

Painting faces

In Egypt, both men and women wore eye make-up. The Egyptians believed that a special black eye-paint, called kohl, had magical healing powers and could cure bad eyesight and fight eye infections.

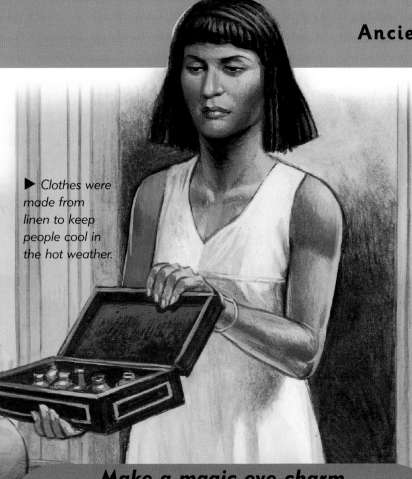

► Clothes were made from linen to keep people cool in the hot weather.

Eye of Horus was a lucky charm worn by Egyptians to bring them good luck.

Wigs were worn by rich people and were often made from human hair!

Reed sandals were made from papyrus.

Make a magic eye charm

You will need
- self-hardening modelling clay
- a length of leather strip or thick cord
- a pencil   • poster paints
- a paintbrush   • varnish

1. Shape the clay into the eye of Horus, shown above. Add extra clay for the pupil of the eye. Add more clay at the top of the charm. Use a pencil to make a loop.
2. Leave the clay to harden.
3. Paint in bright colours and leave to dry. Varnish.
4. Wear your charm for extra luck!

29

The working life

Most people worked as craftworkers or farm labourers. These included carpenters, potters, weavers, jewellers and shoemakers. Scribes were important people in ancient Egypt. Unlike ordinary Egyptians, scribes knew how to read and write. They kept records of everything that happened from day to day.

▶ Children went to schools for scribes where they would learn how to read and write.

Workers often made a living by selling their goods at the market.

A typical lunch for a worker was bread and onions, washed down with beer.

Carpenters made statues and furniture for the pharaoh.

Test your memory!

Can you name the following items from life in ancient Egypt?

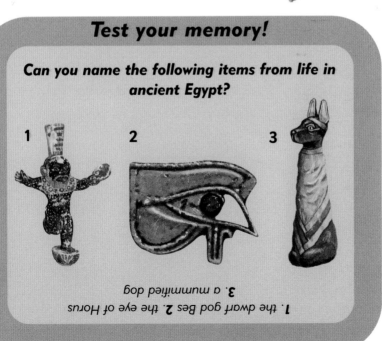

1   **2**   **3**

1. the dwarf god Bes 2. the eye of Horus 3. a mummified dog

Food and fun

Bread was the most important food in the diet of ancient Egypt, and the most popular drink was beer. Banquets were huge parties held by wealthy Egyptians, with plenty of food, music and dancing.

▼ Egyptian banquets were big occasions, with lots of eating, drinking and dancing.

Bread was made from wheat or barley.

Musicians played instruments such as the flute and harp.

Design a banquet menu

There was a huge choice of foods at banquets for wealthy Egyptians. Meats such as duck, gazelle and heron were served. There were fruits and vegetables, pastries and cakes, with beer or wine to drink.

Choose the foods for a banquet and design a colourful menu for your guests.

Dancers were often hired to entertain the guests.

33

Painting words

The ancient Egyptians used a system of picture-writing called hieroglyphics. Each hieroglyph, or picture, represented an object or sound. The insides of many Egyptian tombs were decorated with hieroglyphs, often showing scenes from the dead person's life.

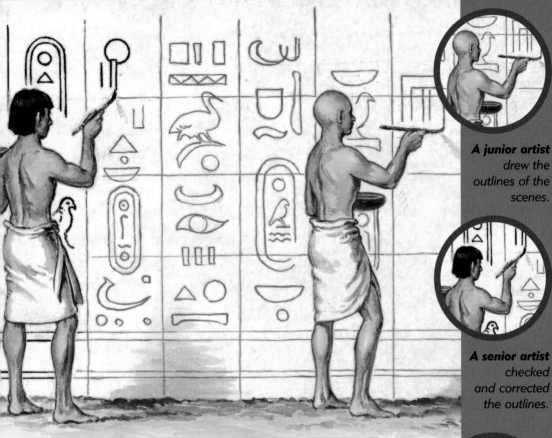

A junior artist drew the outlines of the scenes.

A senior artist checked and corrected the outlines.

A painter filled the outlines in colour.

Write your name in Hieroglyphics

Below you will see the hieroglyphic alphabet. Look at the name written below in hieroglyphs. Can you write yours?

J A N E   W A L K E R

A B C D E F G H I J K L M

N O P Q R S T U V W X Y Z

Egyptian know-how

The ancient Egyptians had many skills.
They not only invented their own alphabet, but they were the first to write on a kind of paper made from papyrus reeds. The Egyptians also used their knowledge of the stars to help build temples. Egyptian doctors understood the basic workings of the human body.

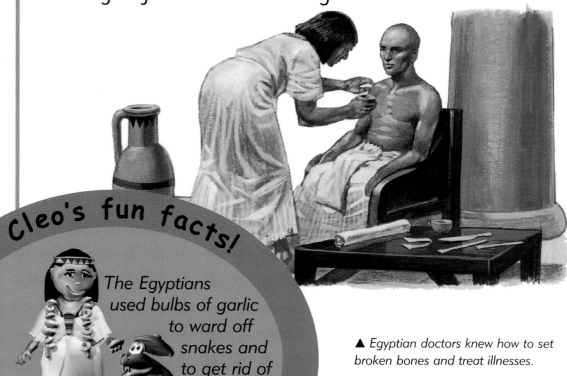

Cleo's fun facts!

The Egyptians used bulbs of garlic to ward off snakes and to get rid of tapeworms from their bodies!

▲ Egyptian doctors knew how to set broken bones and treat illnesses.

▼ *Papyrus was expensive because it took such a long time to make.*

Papyrus scrolls *were the first kind of paper ever used.*

Ink *was made by mixing water with charcoal or coloured minerals.*

1. First people had to cut down the papyrus stems, and cut them into lots of thin strips.

2. Then someone laid these strips in rows on a frame to form layers.

Reed brushes *were used for writing on papyrus.*

3. The papyrus strips were then pressed under weights. This squeezed out the water and squashed the layers together.

4. Finally, when the papyrus was dry, a man with a stone rubbed the surface smooth for writing.

Sports and games

The ancient Egyptians had many different hobbies. Hippo-hunting was a dangerous but popular sport. Hunters in reed boats, armed only with spears and ropes, killed hippos in the Nile. In the desert, hunters chased lions, antelope and wild bulls. At home, the Egyptians enjoyed playing board games.

Make a snake game

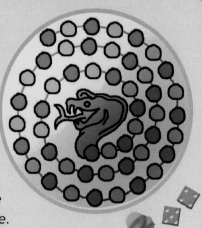

You will need:
- a sheet of thick cardboard
- a large dinner plate
- a paintbrush • scissors
- coloured pens
- white paint • counters
- a pencil • two dice

1. Place the plate on the card and draw round the outside. Cut out the circle.
2. Paint one side white and leave to dry.
3. Draw a snake's head in the centre of the board.
4. Draw small circles spreading out from the centre until you reach the edge of the board. Colour them in.
5. Put a counter for each player on the outside circle. The winner is the first player to reach the snake's head.

Senet may have been the most popular board game.

Amenhotep III was famous for killing over 90 wild bulls on one hunting trip!

Coloured balls were filled with seeds so that they rattled when thrown.

Index